THE THIRTEENTH ANGEL

Born in Cornwall, son of an Estonian wartime refugee, **Philip Gross** has lived in Plymouth, Bristol and South Wales, where he was Professor of Creative Writing at Glamorgan University (USW). His 27th collection, *The Thirteenth Angel* (2022) is a Poetry Book Society Recommendation, and follows eleven previous books with Bloodaxe, including *Between the Islands* (2020), *A Bright Acoustic* (2017); *Love Songs of Carbon* (2015), winner of the Roland Mathias Poetry Award and a Poetry Book Society Recommendation; *Deep Field* (2011), a Poetry Book Society Recommendation; *The Water Table* (2009), winner of the T.S. Eliot Prize; and *Changes of Address: Poems 1980-1998* (2001), his selection from earlier books including *The Ice Factory, Cat's Whisker, The Son of the Duke of Nowhere, I.D.* and *The Wasting Game*. Since *The Air Mines of Mistila* (with Sylvia Kantaris, Bloodaxe Books, 1988), he has been a keen collaborator, most recently with artist Valerie Coffin Price on *A Fold in the River* (2015) and with poet Lesley Saunders on *A Part of the Main* (2018). *I Spy Pinhole Eye* (2009), with photographer Simon Denison, won the Wales Book of the Year Award 2010. He received a Cholmondeley Award in 2017.

His poetry for children includes *Manifold Manor, The All-Nite Café* (winner of the Signal Award 1994), *Scratch City* and *Off Road To Everywhere* (winner of the CLPE Award 2011) and the poetry-science collection *Dark Sky Park* (2018).

PHILIP GROSS

THE
THIRTEENTH
ANGEL

BLOODAXE BOOKS

ISBN: 978 1 78037 635 6

First published 2022 by
Bloodaxe Books Ltd,
Eastburn,
South Park,
Hexham,
Northumberland NE46 1BS.

www.bloodaxebooks.com
For further information about Bloodaxe titles
please visit our website and join our mailing list
or write to the above address for a catalogue.

Supported using public funding by
ARTS COUNCIL
ENGLAND

Cover design: Neil Astley & Pamela Robertson-Pearce.

Printed in Great Britain by Bell & Bain Limited, Glasgow, Scotland, on
acid-free paper sourced from mills with FSC chain of custody certification.

ACKNOWLEDGEMENTS

Acknowledgements are due to due the editors of the following publications in which some of these poems first appeared: *Divining Dante* (ed. Paul Munden, Nessa O'Mahoney et al), *The Friend, Giant Steps* (ed. Paul Munden & Shane Strange), *Long Poem Magazine, The Manhattan Review, The Poetry Review, Poetry Salzburg, Poetry Wales, Raceme, Wales Arts Review*, and *WRITE Where We Are NOW*.

'Sky Space' and 'Moon O' were read by Philip Gross at the BBC Proms in August 2022 broadcast on BBC Radio 3.

'Black Glass Sonata' is a respectful nod to the work in glass of Philip Baldwin and Monica Guggisberg; 'Crack and Warp' does likewise to the 'Crack and Warp Columns' in wood by David Nash.

CONTENTS

Nocturne: The Information
(Finsbury Park, 2018)

Night, wired and ticking. Not a wink
is not electric: sign to sign, the shut shops'
half-sleep; street-
    lights under their hoods;
street-time moving in jolts, red, red-
amber, green
    and the cold blush of blue
on a cheek: stranger, her mobile tingling
with presence. Passing.
       Voices quick-
timed between nodes of light.

*

From my third floor window,
the park's null, an amnesia amongst us
but for this,
    a petty funfair's glitter
fidgeting, its garlands of bare bulbs
draped round a throb
      from which only
the chittery wavelengths rise to here.
The two-armed spinner-ride
       goes on trying
to bowl itself, its squealing pods, away;

*

On a tidemark of light, the road beyond
the park, at intervals, the dim stacked
blocks of pixels
    that are buses, homebound.

Faces, bits and bytes, in them, reprogrammed
stop by stop.
                We are the information.
Bin lorry, police car, bus: their roofs are coded
for the sky to read,
                and me, from here.
A live flow diagram. The pulse of us.

*

Bank Holiday heat stokes up the street sound,
windows open, people expanding to, beyond,
the borders of their bodies.
                We are too much
to take in, the night air a relish of spice
and charred meat,
                burger, best kebabs
in London, Roti Joupa Caribbean Takeaway.
We're all night taxi, never quite
                the last bus.
We're too much to fit into the livelong day.

*

Chance collocations... Like the beat someone
you'll never meet has timed their pulse to
in a passing car.
                Like light: the sun that's going,
has gone, where we are... in the same moment flares
from every window
                of the flicker of a train
at speed, into the half-shade of this room,
a grand old cinema projector
                juddering,
the celluloid smouldering, about to catch flame.

*

12

To get it whole, a world unframed except for this
which could be any window: its never-quite-
right angles – farm lane
                    become high street, cut
by rail embankment – our never quite parallel lines,
our margins of error.
                    Brambles, billboard, fast food shack,
particular, equal. To share the mutual respect of things.
Like God's eye view. To see
                    as we'd be seen,
each one of us, each half-filled rubble sack.

*

Immaculately unconcerned by my or any
looking, the van-yard's breeze-block office
has a night-light, on
                    at all hours. No one
ever comes or goes. The seventeen
(believe me)
                    stained translucent skylights
on its flat roof are unripe pagodas. Red skip,
six, sometimes seven
                    vans as white as swans.
How not to love this? Let me count the ways.

*

Voices and footfall, falling leaves, or do I mean
lives – the near- and never-quite-a repetition
of us that lays down a city.
                    The breath of it,
in, out, the catch of new consonant sounds
on the street – the Voiceless
                    Uvular Fricative
of Arabic, one you feel at the back of the cave

of the mouth
               yet have no sign for. So we sense
the drift of continents, wind on the waters between.

*

A stringy waist-high palm tree, unaccountably
alive... Between it and the spear-spike fence,
and rail yard gate
               that dumb-clunks open,
shut at all hours, a mess of bin sacks, cardboard
buckling with wet,
               a nest (I witnessed this,
an act of grace) the road sweepers skirt round.
From it, at dawn,
               a man unfolded, straightened
what appeared to be a tie, and walked away.

*

A place that's a perch on the tingling wires
of connection. See the Tube map, the Overground
ghosted in
               like lymph among the bloodstream,
bus routes clustered to a node: here. Now overlay
the map of shadows.
               Show what slammed door,
night flit, what missed foothold or chill current
in a track-marked vein
               leads here, under the bridge,
washed up on cardboard. What darkening flood.

*

...as if one of the culverted rivers, swollen
to a gush, had ripped open a seam at our feet,

an edge of crumbling
                    that we have to seem
not to see, in the weary end- or bleary start-
of-workday rush.
                    The underworld's arranged
not in circles but parallel: bus lane, cycle track,
walkway and,
                    motionless, the sleepers-in-
the-daytime, when it's safer. Some worse than asleep.

*

Above, dull gunfire. In the iron-girdered cave,
all-day-dark and always dripping,
one of the newspaper nests
                    is empty.
In that absence, people have left gifts: apple.
Orange. A granola bar.
                    Health food.
To make a votive offering to the borderline-
departed, that's one thing;
                    another, to pass it
hand to hand, eye to eye, with one of the shades.

*

The comfort of trains in the night. Non stop
to the North. Wherever – but the shuttle-clack
of it, the fact
                    that it goes on, the shuddery
whack-whack on the girders, over the rough-
sleeping underworld
                    of under-bridge,
hourly. Above as below, faces lit in the zip-
lighter fizz of passing.
                    And all manner of things
shall be tickety-boo. Tickety-boo. Tickety-boo.

15

*

Out of body – of the body of the city,
not soaring, just three storeys, more the low
swoop of an angel
                    or the shite-hawk kites
street-sweeping London in an age of plague.
Come midnight
                    the delivery truck is below,
rattling its cages, orange hazard-flashers
twitching to and fro.
                    It is feeding the shop,
our sudden appetites, at all hours. Want it now.

*

One storey down, across the street, another
cast of lives. Grey-blue and flickering the in-
house twilight of TV.
                    Thin curtains half fastened,
as he is, shrugged out on the sofa, undone
from his day self,
                    anyone. Her face, from this
hard angle, never seen. Snooper, stalker, spook,
fly on the wall, pass-
                    over angel, we are abjected
by surveillance – the see-er as much as the seen.

*

A grand thing, out of sight, that surge and fall-
back on the sound horizon, above and beyond
the quiver-breath of traffic,
                    the petty maracas
of the small trains, sirens now and then.
Match day today.

They say it's all we need
of love and battle and belonging, of *Yes!*
/ *no-o-o-o*... safely caged
in a game. A glow
like glory. Crash now, like huge weather, rising sea.

*

The unconscious of the city isn't in
its history. No ghosts. That's our nostalgia
for the always-
slipping of *now*
from our grip; our faith that somewhere
it still lodges,
any given present;
some ledge of pastness has broken its fall.
Potsherd, cracked pipe,
whatever's femur,
join the same queue in the ever-underground,

*

the near-motionless rush hour, the dumb
all-voice-at-once, of soil or hardcore:
refugees
without a word of the language
of mineral Now, assimilating to its buzz
or crumble. Or
sometimes, a little proud,
a broken edge sticks – accent, topknot,
sidelock our attention
snags on: an itch
in the moment of the city's calloused skin.

*

Awake too early, and too late
to go back to bed. Instead, sit with this low
suffusion coming through
                    a thin cloud-cover,
pink: nobody's rosy fingers but a grander thing,
the bending of the edge
                    of always-
sunlight round this rock, in its cocoon
of restless gases.
                    Against it, Stamford Hill's
skyline, laid bare in nit-picking silhouette.

*

The cranes are of one mind. They know, even asleep,
the direction of wind – of least resistance. To turn
and yet hold to the upright.
                    Thus the Orthodox
in their side curls (next year in Jerusalem,
always; last year, Lithuania)
                    or the qibla app
that never forgets Mecca. Red lights at the tips
of the jibs: less a machine
                    in Sleep mode
than marker buoys on a treacherous sea.

*

High-rise is a pale stalk, only tenuously
fed by the ground. Its wires and ducts
where sap flows
                    snapped so easily.
Is a penthouse a reach for the sky
or a flight from the ground?
                    Commanding
heights, yes, if by money and choice; if not,
an exile,

solitary/crowded, unseen/in full view
of the somehow-lost country below.

*

Lights in the low cloud like red tethered stars.
There is an upper storey to the night. Dim-
dark on darker,
          the outlines of cranes are mere
force fields created by our looking, our believing:
the minimal grace
          that holds them in the middle air,
their higher mathematics, QED, between the flight
paths we etch onto heaven
                    and the constellations
and the mess of fallen light called here.

*

The closer to blackout, the trimmer the curtains'
fit, the more precise the image through the chink.
In this camera obscura
                    we retreat to sleep,
wake to a shock of light, blue riffling backwards,
like a fanned wing,
          like a case of knives.
Outside, a roadblock: hazard lights, blue spinners
juggling their panic.
          We may be the news,
an incident, already. Or not. It's too soon to tell.

*

As if seen from the edge, the ledge without
dimensions between flash and blast, the skid-
bite of tyres
          mounting the pavement, or the sky-

blank of ward window, or any last where,
the more precious because
                              it could be, therefore
is, the world... To grasp one thing: a thread of hair
come loose behind a stranger's
                              ear, a shred
of a jingling ring-tone. Time. I could go on...

*

Old stories come back from the dead – of soul
as guest, at worst as hostage in the body –
turned truer,
                now we are the information?
I don't mean the posthuman, uploaded to life
as a meme, as everlasting
                          me-me, but the flow
seen from a great remove (our selves as shoal,
as murmuration)
                catching light, rippling through
these streets, this flesh, this temporary habitation.

*

Out-of-body: not yet a divorce for the soul,
more of a trial separation. Looking down.
That's you,
            disappearingly small
among raw cluttered decks of the tower-tops,
shafts, wires,
                heating vents, lift-engines
as if we had to wear our workings somewhere
away from each other, a wound
                              that must heal open,
trusting it to the sky and passing aeroplanes.

*

All this, the perceptible city, tingling. Now
isn't the time for *I-sing-the-body-electric*
ecstasies. Sing
        the body that's weary,
sleepless, and a little scuffed, at 3 a.m.,
and afloat, in the long view,
                above dark
scrubland, dark marshes: no city at all,
except for electricity.
             Lights on the surface
like will o' the wisps. Sing simultaneity…

*

all this, all together, in the eyes of… Let's
not go as far as *God*, but the quiet angels
of the Internet. Not
            the glitter-sprites
of data but the patient pools of space between,
the shade of a palm tree
           in deserts
of digital light. They watch, with no message
for us
      who are too much the message already.
Simply presence, with us. Simply listening.

Porcelain

I don't know
what kind of perfect crockery
Pangaea was, the mono-continent,

before God's whim
to send it splintering – what tiff of God
with God's self
                    or what decadent
aesthetic shivered it, setting the sea
in the rifts as *kintsugi*,
                    as glittering gold.

Or what dismay,
what fascination, as they widened,
with tide-heave, with storm-whorls, with tsunamis...

Or was God
already too busy with His/Her/Their own
splintering
                    into pronouns,
all sharp-edged and glinting, to notice
the shattering crust,
                    the great
subductions back as if Mother Magma
could put it together again,
                    and bird flocks

scattering, up
into light, armies arrayed as for battle,
rubble cancelling equations of whole cities,

and Spring
like a glorious rash across a continent,

and the great souk,
                    Samarkand,
and spices, strange diseases and the stolen
craft of porcelain
                    and love, and years,
the lost tracks in the sand, or ploughed field
where the harrow
                    turns over one,
two, fragments of a plate's rim, the family best?
And us.
            All the Ten Thousand Things.

The Follies

Slipping out of the City
in a grey-brown fug,
air full of uncompleted rain.

Behind us, already reduced
to the ghosts of themselves,
the follies of big money:

gherkin, protuberant shapes
of the time. Only the shard
is honest: cloud-capped

splinters. The final push
to the summit... called off
at the snowfield of Forever.

On the way down,
that (statistics tell us)
is when climbers die.

Smatter

Sometimes he looks in the mirror and this is what he sees:

a smattering on the windscreen, like a slash of hail
on the cusp between sharpness and slush
                              or the drift
of small long-legged things, the spread wings, the critical moment,

or flyaway seeds that lift
                              off the hedgerow in the dry gust
that's his own speed. He blinks and it's gone

for now at least. What remains is his momentum
going forward
                              but in free fall. Travelling.

*

Partitas and fugues
by many hands in many keys
played simultaneously...

which is how we might hear
the ant swarm, the gnat dance,
our own dissolution, were

we not such slaves to the small
but driven god Direction.

*

So that was the career plan, and modest enough: to be
the curator of the chaff of things, all
the blown-away moments that nobody saw:

the inclination of that grass blade in the wind, the lift
and nearly flare of that was it a bird, no,
a polythene bag whipped up by the slipstream.

A curator... just one of the lesser order of recording angels.
Why not? The grand ones have a lot on their minds, or
what used to be minds before the white-out of omniscience.

*

Road movies... This isn't a landscape where you see the distances
unfurl, the straight aim across prairie, into dust, red desert, sunset

or any illusion of the gold land just beyond the ever-after (its glow
now and then silhouetting one tree, one cactus, or deserted shack).

We are bound for the ferry port. There'll be queues. And questions.
We are bound for the border (hardening) defined as where a story

stops. A pane where things in flight get spattered, flat.

*

Overwrite me, he once whispered to the world
– some kind of adolescent rapture, he forgets –

as if he was the world's blank jotter.
And like the wryly vengefully responsive fates

in a Greek myth, it proceeded. What
you ask for, be prepared to have
for ever,
            much more than enough.

*

After the places with names, the ones
he or his smartphone will remember,
now:
     in the hiatus between here and when,
between holiday and history, the children in the back
or maybe just the memory of them,
                    it begins, he
/she begins, as if this was a *bardo*, a between-life:
now, next, after this, who will I be?

*

          So the journey goes on,
the sense perceptions pelter on the retina
too fast to erase,
          their traces cross-hatched denser,
the pressure of their tiny impacts rammed
to a brillo-pad mass, abrasion,
               and on
until no optic nerve remains unsated,
no space remains to move through,
             time
itself too full to move, no gaps between.

*

Lamp post. Lamp post, lamp post,
with their melancholy down-regard.

Fin de siècle aesthetes, elegantly pained
by us – *how banal, look, a car,
and a car* – quite unaware

how their own pose is identical,
in hundreds, and equally spaced,

all the way to a horizon
they will never raise their heads to see.

*

Imagine every glance, however
sidelong, through however wincing-thin
the crack –
                a fractious child's
                                between the megaliths
of his own boredom
                        or his mum's / his dad's
abutting silences;
                what slips into a breath
between two lover's sudden bickering
they can't explain;
                        or the miles streaming back
east through the grille in the container
with its undeclared cargo of hope,
with scarcely air enough for one,
let alone the twenty, huddled, let alone
the world...
                Imagine each glance
impacted, laid and overlaid
to textures like mute polished marble,
time cross-sectioned, all the tiny
lives, the tiny
                deaths, displayed

*

The plainchant of speed. The monks, the truckers,
in their high cabs, or their satnavs, telling the names

of Europe over, till the words mean nothing; there is only
flow and eddy, mattins, evensong, the rise and fall.

*

My god, how many fields does it take
to make a distance? And (we need this
sorted out before a real eternity sets in)
which is more terrible: the countlessness
of trite half-acres (drive-time radio,
its short attention span)?
                           Or the one
without horizons, ever-after, featureless
except for the arrow on the map: *You Are Here?*

*

Cloud shadows over the fields. How many ways
to spell weather, or the shapes of shadows
melting over, into our roads, our walls, our
arbitrary lines of demarcation.
                                 Stopped
at the border, what can shadows say? Melt
shadows into shadows. In the lorry park,
to sleep or cling between the axles,
              in the cargo hold,
                                  how many languages
in which to lose your face and name...

*

When a straggle of cranes came over,
on a slipstream of migration,
                 necks and legs stretched out
as if to stretch the sky itself, to make it wide enough
for everyone who needs it,

I was driving in the opposite direction.
Something they were fleeing from was where I had to go.

*

A prayer, if you will,
for Alexandru, in his 40-tonner
out of Bucharest,
pushed to the edge
of his legal drive time
then a little further
to the lethal single kilometre more beyond.

*

Big buzzard on a fence post
like a canny hunch. He is counting us by,
        or in, or out. Whatever,
there's a rendezvous he has in mind.

Not us, now. Now, he gives up waiting.
Rises, gathering armfuls, wingfuls
        of his patience, heavy
as it is. Becomes a single shrug in feathers.

Off, first up the air's steep stairs until
the thermal takes him, and we fall
        away beneath, a detail
in his high perspective, dwindling.

*

Wind in the wheat field: it knows all
about big data: how we feature in it, me and you
as diminishing points, our voices hushed in awe

as vast patterns emerge, the big beasts
crunching though the undergrowth
in which we scuttle, or are crushed.

*

Service station: where the spirits of the un-place
        you will never come to
                        except passing
            sit down for a break, for a breather
        if these things had breath, for a quick
eternal cappuccino, with the spirits of the other
        places left or longed for,
                                smoke shapes
strung out, fading, in the spaces in between.

*

The road has dispensed with all directions
other than its own. It gives the lie
to the lie of the land,

time likewise. Only, now and then
catch a glimpse of a small stream
cut into a culvert's dark

on one side, vanished under. Its will
to go somewhere, some compulsion
white lines can't rule, road signs can't translate.

*

A prayer for the small ones
on their flightpaths – song thrush,
lapwing, as the earth's tilt tips them,
skylark, woodcock, plover,
                                curlew
cut from the sky, its long cry
flying on without it.

A prayer for the mute
weight of the wild boar piglet
rolled to the hard shoulder.
For the badger.
                    For the roadside
strips, stray clumps the wild
wood has come to, from which they
the homeless ones broke cover, centuries ago.

*

A meditation on the moment: visualise
this space in the air, a moment after
your own passing through it, the moment before
the car behind you fills that space precisely,
somebody else's eyes blink, thinking
this same thought, that moment: here
I am   am I   am here.

*

Mist, out of nowhere.
                    It's as if the ink
with which to draw the world, to give it edges,
ran out, and the pigment to colour it in.
We hit it, with no impact
                              but a falling
feeling. Sideways, all around us, white-grey
swirling flow, with almost shapes, with
shadows in it
                    that our headlights throw
from shapes that we seem not to see,
much less can we explain.

*

Peering into the press and pebbledashing of sensations,
each one a scratch on the lens, crack
in the windscreen which will catch the light,

there are landscapes emerging, like an older
painting leaching through the plastered wall,

another country with its folds, bourns, darkwoods,
songlines. Your long walking there.

Wild geese out of the north, in season, still
with the ice sheet at their backs, come calling
their reminders, almost too high for us to hear.

*

A page of this, unwritten / written in the waking
of the night. When he looks in the morning,
          nothing... Or there may be
a ghost of itself, like archaeology, the page
microscopically trodden, like a footpath in the dew
          left two millennia ago. Accept it, this
may be the point. I mean, what if the road
took it upon itself to remember
          everything, us and
our passings, one by one by one.

*

If the road has a voice, it's the rip-sigh of tyres on tarmac,
voice as real as a river's, also flickering with small facets
of reflection in the light,
                    with every word, in every car,
on every mobile, preserved: a white, white-water sound.
Silence itself could not be calmer or more grand.

*

The paradox, which is the grandchild
    of a paradox: the road
is going nowhere / the road
    is nothing but a going.
Ask the river, it could tell you. Now
ask it again. Ask the same river twice.

*

I am here am here am I. And now, and now. In ink,
in insect-flicker and smear
we have an illustration of how far

it is beyond us, what we conceive to be
the eye of God, that sees all this (and
now, and now again)

as one, as shape, a space-and-time-piece,
which those hands, if it had hands, could turn
to catch the light at every angle. We

approximate, speed smearing bush, bush,
road sign, faster while that further tree,
that wind-vane, slide by slower –

to the skyline where one silhouette
stands motionless. Most probably,
but who knows, it's not God.

*

A prayer for Alice, alone

with her quarrelsome three
in the back, strapped in
    to the wrangle and shove

of themselves with each other,
an hour to Calais at least and no
we can't stop we'll miss
        the ferry and why
can't they won't they won't
they just
                              until
she turns her head a moment

that's the end of it.

*

This smatter on the windscreen,
it's the price we pay for speed,
for getting somewhere. Wipers
whimpering – their slush and wheeze
as they push back at the pelting
rain-splats, each shivering out
into distortion – in season (can
it be that time already?) the seductive
lacework, crumpling itself by degrees, of first snow.

*

This be the book. The one
page. Not the holy text, the highest, but
the one we wrote together,
                              from the first
dumb scratch to great machineries
of syntax, glassy chimes of concepts,
                                        the shoal
switching sometimes right-left, sometimes
left-right, sometimes breaking into flicker-bits
till they arrived
                      at everywhere, the page

we call the Present. This
                              is not it
but a crude facsimile I made an age ago.

*

From the sky's point of view
or from a boulder's, the road
is a muscle, always flexing.
The road is a verb, as electricity

is all verb, not the individual
atoms, nouns, you/me, our
indecisions, alternating currents
switching to and fro.

*

Could this in passing also
be a love song? Road is all
             relationship, the traffic
             between things, between
us. Breath, touch, word
and matter, the quiver and hum
             even at night, the glow
             behind the skyline. Road
is what connects us. Road
is appetite, and need. What some
             will give their lives for. (A prayer
             for Zaid and his sons, trusting
their savings to a man in Thessaloniki
for the idea of Europe. For all
             the others who had nothing
             left to give, not even names.)
Road is a prayer in tarmac
                              to escape

from what comes after them, to live
in some direction, to recover what's been lost.

*

Sometimes it comes to us, with eyes shut, white
lines still unreeling at and into us and through:
that this
        is how it's always been. How always
          is. An always
travelling.
Travelling.   Still.   Still
               travelling.

A Q'ran of Ruzbihan

(16th century, Shiraz, in the Chester Beatty Library, Dublin)

Like opening the door on the weaver's shop,
on a whirr and shuddering of looms

that weave words, those words of all words,
like the rarest thread – at just the right tension,

so no syllable, no sign
be overstrained and snap, and none hang limp...
                    Day-in-day-out industry

in the writing room: first the calligrapher,
then the pattern-maker, the colourist, in turn,

the page slipping smoothly as water to the weir's
edge, its designs steady as those of the sky

reflected, willows
of the garden of all gardens trailing fronds in it,
                    the weaver, meanwhile, muttering

the threads beneath his breath, as if they were
his breaths, and them breathing him

for as long as they are unfinished, his hands moved
by the taut threads, by the symmetries emerging.

Hands cannot be weary as long
as they keep pace with the way the text is flowing,
                    how the Recitation runs.

Believe them: we might live for ever if we never
left our work, the one work that will never be done.

Black Glass Sonata

1

Transparency
is the most commonplace of glass's

propositions. *Ob*-viously... But black

glass...? Beadlets
like a lightning strike might leave

in open desert. Black pearls. Convex drops

dispersing your reflection
to all corners of the room; also the abolition

of all corners. Black glass. Suspicion

of black mirror.
It sees you as much as it's seen through.

2

For now we see through [or: *in*]
a glass, darkly... Our translations

waver on that point
as we ourselves waver, candle-shadows,
as glass too will always be translation; so the great
East window translates ordinary daylight, bruised with weather,

into glory.
It would do the same for us.

But glass that is neither a pane nor a container,
any more than the fine bulb at the tip
of ice-melt, ripening into its
moment, its fall...

To say what it *holds* might be to leave
the word, too, hanging at the brink of wordlessness.

3

These black glass held-breaths with their lips sealed: a high
and dark art, to create a thing that does not need us,
as remote as the moment of meeting, of actually meeting,
an animal's eye...

4

We know the timbre of the glass harmonica,
its ethereal glimmering whine
just playing at the skyline of our hearing, there and nowhere,
like the Northern Lights. Now

consider the same, only black.

5

In the room of a hundred glass presences
there is one (I can't swear whether it even exists
or is implied by all the others)
that I want to touch

and dare not,

as if it might be still hot
with the knowledge of its forging, that it can't forgive,
the way some children can't forgive their parents. It might be cold

enough to burn the skin or gaze, like Arctic night.
Or balancing, dark angel on a pinhead.
It might shatter at my crude

intrusion if I miss

the point: that
it's a squint, a glimpse: slit window
into the place, as Rilke says of lovers' solitudes,

I have to guard and am not meant to be.

Scenes from the Lives of Stone Angels
(Armagh Cathedrals)

Whether stained glass or an altar screen, they press
themselves into its plane, their wings packed round them,

                                                        press

against this box of hallowed space we're in...

                                        though not
to burst it (Pre-Raphaelite faces too tranquil for that).

If we were to believe those raptor pinions,

                                        then the smack
of them against the glass would be a shattering.

Or they'd be stun-flung, gasping in the yard, like pigeons
from the made-for-humans picture pane,

                                        the holy trace

revealed by light would be a waxy wing-flare, fanned
to its up-tilted tips

                        and where the face

might be, a smear, a shock, a turned
cheek as from (I wince

                        too, saying this)

a blow

            that says it's kindness
or God's kiss.

*

An everyday
annunciation. It's what he does. She's plump,
a little lumpish, at the pious stage

and hunched with kneeling
though the open book she's been distracted from
must be empty –

it's her story-to-be, after all –

while he's her unarguable grace,
the way he arches over, a shape her humility fits,
and he's lovely, of course –

trust me, his bedside manner says –
with his vestments of wing all ruched behind him, crisp
as if somebody ironed them this morning,

somebody waved him off to work.

*

Stump angels
that one of the lost
count of burnings and sackings left as relic –
                    unintended cross

left by the punching out
of windows, blunt X buttressed
by two blunter figures in flight, all distinguishing
                    features erased,

sand-blasted by their dogged flight
through stone and centuries, their opposite
momentums, till all that remains

is limb buds; their faces are blanks
to be filled. Aged to a place beyond
age. They could be waiting to be born.

Disintegration Loops

The Disintegration Loops, five hours of ambient music created
by William Basinski from decaying magnetic tape recordings,
New York, September 2001

Our ageing, heard as music... Take a few strands frayed
from another decade, from easy-listening airwaves,

part of the infinitesimal vast squander
(streetlight is the least of it), the whisper-chitter

of us that's spreading out, world without end,
spilling news of ourselves to the light-years' listening ear.

Past saving... One fish of the innumerable
shoal drift-netted from forgotten drive-times,

take four bars, say, this sigh
of lyric strings, spliced end to end;
        they will never reach home

unless home is here – ferrite
chasing its tail around a track of plastic,

the magnetic fidget in its molecules
played, replayed like an afterlife,

to be and to be itself, its self flaking,
decaying – iterations like the same day seen,

re-seen (stepping out from the studio loft
they saw Manhattan's rush reduced

to furls of stillness, debris-dust
of the towers like slow smoke, conjecture
        and the helicopters circling)

each time round the hiss, the fizz,
the crackle closing in... Don't ever suppose

that the antithesis of our lives,
even our words, is silence; feel the fullness

of the silence this brings, listening
as wave on wave of it, this crumbling

un-music like the sea's one gesture
endlessly reprised, take, take again,

breaks on the shingle in a chill haar,
drag and draining through the rubble of us,
rising still, right to our feet.

Moon, O

true moon, if you love us,
 give us nothing. Blank us. Don't
disclose a wink of water, not a glitter-speck of ore –
  nothing to raise a twinkle
  in the futures market's eye. Chaste
goddess (did you have an inkling, all this time, of our
cracked yearnings, how we would madden ourselves,
  how girn in your direction vaguely?)
  stay that way – a glimpse
of pure negation, so not us, not ours, so unwarmed
  to our touch, unstirred by the least
   wind or whim.
  Don't let us think, not
  for a moment, we can have you.
Leave those toddler-suited astronauts slack-dangled
  in their old home movies,
  like marionettes in the wardrobe,
a childhood we'd better forget. Leave the tangled
tracks of our million-dollar toys where they crawled
  to a halt amidst the perfect pointlessness
   of you. O bleachy-
skinned cool mistress, arsenic complexion, dead-
 pan geisha unmoved by our high romance,
  all the shadow-puppetry
  we made of you, O
  pocked and harrowed cheek, no wonder,
those rough-sleeping nights on the sidewalk of space, O
  never really mistress,
  tell us to sling our hook, to blast
and fizzle off, remember we've got family at home.

Sky Space

1

Egg within egg within egg,
sphere within sphere
           cracked open
by Copernicus... What we found outside
was so much almost nothing.
                  Year by year,
look further, and the vertigo will deepen.

2

Where does *sky* become *space*? When
did this happen?
            The first high flight
to break the illusion of blue, to see the air
that we mistook for clarity
                  as a tide,
a shoreline, foam receding at your feet?

3

We had always had night, and stars,
another revelation
               as different from day
as dream from waking. In both, the sense
that *it*, the mystery, is drawing close.
                  In fact,
the sky has gone immeasurably far away.

4

Praise be, the new psalmist might sing,
to the radio telescope array,

                          the thin skies
of the Atacama, those rapt watchers,
for they show us the heights

                                into which
we might fall, depths to which we might rise.

The Mishnah of the Moment

Do you remember when the moment was
itself – now – framed by nothing
but itself?
      You do? Then
    already it's not; from here
on, it's the lovely annotations, scholar
bending closer

as the little light of history, the garret
candle, flutters… is snuffed
before the ink
      dries or the last
    tick of a diacritic fidgets
into place. The scholar leans close,
over, we now see,

the dandruffed shoulder of another
scholar, and another; so the tide
mark rises, or
           is it a falling
    strews this beautifully
tooled tangle, blackened weed-script
on the stones

while at the always and recedingly small
heart of the page, a postage stamp
or single
      data-byte or less,
    the moment dwindles into deep
night-sky perspective, a radio pulse,
a cri de coeur

in language we have to believe
some planet only known
by its bothering
                of the orbit
        of its far star may receive
a thousand years from now. From
now. From now.

Psalm: You

who can number the waves on the sea, and each
wave, say where it began... number likewise the beat

of each heart, my mud-pulse in my cupped hand *and* the tremor-tick
in the breast of the greenfinch, found stunned

by the stroke of wrong sky that was our window... the quickening
too, number that, of the pulse on the scan,

the clump of cells still undecided – to be bird or fish or mammal...
to number their count till the end (would we wish

to know that, of ourselves or the ones by our side?)... who tolerate
our counting rhymes, child to child in the dark,

our itch to call a wave a wave, discrete, as if we believed
in a moment when a thing becomes a thing

distinct from the whole ocean, seamlessness which You, if
we can use the word at all, must surely see, or be.

Paul Klee: the Later Angels

Some of his finest, final angels
are not bodies at all.
Nor 'spirit'. They are the intersections of the things –

shapes, colour-bodies, masses –
that make up the world.
Shift the angle of viewing, the angel is gone.

And yet, once seen, it
is. You could say an illusion.
An annunciation, all the same.

*

The opposite of Rilke's angels
of the (unbearable) absolute, his
are in transit, in transition,

in a rough translation of themselves

as if we had a glimpse inside the chrysalis.
Their word is 'noch', Still Ugly... Still
Groping... Still Female... – their habitation,

in-between. Like us, Unfinished...

In The Making... Not Yet Trained In Walking...
they're reflections on the interface between
our contradictions: the foibles, the fears

and the failings, the reaching beyond.

*

Barely more than a sketch,
a scratch mark of a winged thing – disappointing,
you say – a try-out or reject... Or could you be wrong –
not just about this but evolution
as the ascent of the mount
of plenitude, every last detail known?

No, consider a culture that grew less and less
explicit, the art of understanding spreading
till the least hint of a nod
was manifesto, metaphysics,
rhapsody. By the time the squadrons
of the new times rumbled in,

their team-leaders walked through the streets
and thought them deserted,
sat down, put their feet up in the temples,
filled the space with martial music,
felt obscurely empty,
oh, and couldn't say why.

*

There is no one in the studio but us

and Klee, his back to us, stiffening, bent close
as a tracker on the trail of, following, the pencil's tip.

And somewhere in the space between
our curiosity, his concentration,
an angel occurs.

*

No, don't suppose he waits a lifetime for the moment
                          to bring down an angel to the page

with the fine desperation of the man with one last chance –
he knows he's dying –

tightening the taut gut to reel in the catch. What comes
is a flurry of angels – not

a host; no one could herd these to a chorus – just a twitch
of a pen on the page

and here's another. Brought to earth. They're grounded
and still, but a flittering stillness,

a motionless point around which the whole world
is a shuddering – as if the bird,

in mid air, was the fixed thing and the rip-scudding cloud,
the turbulent hill-scape below,

were trying to take flight, take fright, together. He sighs.
Another angel, placed aside

and numbered. The year, 1939. Not long now.
Now, the sterner angels come.

Ash Plaint in the Key of O

O, ash tree,
bark like hammered pewter
with its dints of lichen, with your opening to high
light, moving, milling, fencing pale blades, leaves beyond
our counting, multiplying themselves (O higher
mathematics) beyond thinking,
on a dazzle of sky;

you are a play of permutations
your material, its tensile strength, the way
you tense and sway against eddy and curl of weather,
its fluid dynamics that move like a mind
of their own (O spacious
contemplator) driven

by the swing and sweat
of the unconscious globe. All this:
leaf, light and wind, tree, me, a tumble-mill
of collocations, now and then resolving
to a round sound, an almost-
a-word – to an *oh!*

*

Oh, ash tree,
In the same breath, two days later,
I notice a twig, not on you, grande dame, you light-shuffler
but the pushy upstart in the hedge, a thruster
for the daylight – one twig withering.
Its own already-Autumn

on a mere sapling: tips
droop, crisp and shrivel. Dieback.

The word flits like a shadow-bird amongst the leaves
leaving only its call: *gone, gone.* The young
succumb, the well-established old
die slowly. Knowingly.

And now I know,
I see the twigs, whole branches even,
that you're readying to shed. To sacrifice.

And all the glory-play with light
is glorying still but: oh,
ash, O ash,
oh...

Transient

Blown out of the sky
as if a sleeve of wind
had snagged on barbed wire

or as if a pot of storm
had boiled over, scattering flock-
froth over fields and gardens,

discohered – one redwing

here, a little dazed, palpably
not quite itself, its whole
self being in the flock, the taut

lines of connection (today, torn
or tangled) that slingshot them
across the sky, connect them

to the old horizons (gone).

A Near Distance

The mutterings of quiet circumstance
under the threshold of attention. Now,
in the stilled house, hear their breathing. Lives, almost,

you share your space with. The dogged snore,
like sleeping uphill, of a washing machine
mid-cycle. A tap upstairs coughs on, umm-errs, chokes off.

Attend to them. Your life and those you love
hang on this patient servitude. How the wind
puts its shoulder to the wheeler-dealing of the wind farm

with its dumb gesticulations; how precisely
we can calibrate a slice of hell
turning ore to sheet metal; how well smog can conceal

the barefoot scurry into sweatshops,
     in rackety silence, at first light, in cities
we can't put a name to – white noise, dirtied slightly,

that translates as multitudes. It washes though.
     Forgetfulness. It's a catch in the throat
of storm drains. Gutters frothing. Rusty outfalls. In the dark,

the flicker of the broadband router
     dreaming your life into being. The wink of it,
a marker light far out in the sea lanes near dangerous shoals.

The Named Storm

...there, beside me, me and three or four
cold others on the hopeless platform, each of them with names
I'd never know,
the named storm waiting, sullen, with us,
with late getting later, and the indicator board
out of excuses. Could this have been our doing: we had called her
by name?

Now it's night; I'm home; the named storm too
is home; she's roaming round the garden – not a single flood
of presence but the here-and-there of her, one moment
in the alley round the back, bad-whispering;
the next,
in the trees like a flock of herself, dispersed along the branches
and ready to fly, with her hundred mile cries.

No consolation
to be told that soon she'll have blown herself out,
nor-nor-east; that she'll be losing her identity, off somewhere
I too am forgetting, some cape, some ness, some Viking
vowel,
to be a crackle in our radio reception, the lights
flickering, her absence still more *here* for being named.

Developing the Negatives

1

That's the real thing, you said, the negative, still slick and fragrant from its bath of developing fluid. That's the original. The thing itself. Where do we go for that now, in the cloud-world of digital, in which every moment disperses at once, into data, a whole sum of pluses and minuses, like a scattered ant-heap, at the speed of light? Entropy in a box, very portable. Look, we can have everything. But not to touch.

2

The black, though, of these photo prints... Something other than lightless – rather, soft matt black I want to stroke, expecting a fine nap like velvet. Or to find it feel like soot so fine it flows like liquid, only dry.

3

Pure black takes all that light can offer. And takes it to keep. Takes gratefully – there's nothing grasping in this. (Remember, white is not light-friendly. White rejects light... which is why light comes to us). Black, though... An open house. And a warm hearth, where that energy comes in and is translated, light to heat.

4

Black: not the enemy of light. More its dancing partner... Not what snuffs out vision, but what gives it definition, edges, shape. And depth, too, in its mouldings and perspective. Light is all surface. Soon enough, we tire of it, and begin to long for dark, its inwardness.

5

Half truth at best, to call photography *writing with light*. It's in the shadow that the mass of things resides. Their secret life.

6

Dark matter: the undisclosed heart, into which telescopes reach as clumsily as blind man's buff... The basement storey of the iceberg of the universe, without which none of this would float.

7

Nor is space dark. Rather, an unimpeded thoroughfare for the wavelengths. If not, if there was impediment, or even friction (see the atmosphere, that precious brittle bowl we see as blue), then we would call it something. We would call it light.

8

Eclipse: no denying the awe of it. To stand in the mouth of its cave... Yet it's only a matter of standpoint. Half of us are, at any time, eclipsed... and we do what? Sleep through it, mostly.

9

Imagine this: that the white space we so lovingly construct around the poem is the poem's shadow. Not its absence, but its (no, not identical) twin.

10

There's nothing passive about them, shadows. More energetic than we are, they stretch and flex and shrink. Like a dog off the leash, they streak out from us and back, back. Later, they lie down beside us, faithfully. Even in the deep of night, they don't run off, with their feral companions. (Or do they? How would we know?)

11

It's no accident: I write this in black notebooks. OK, white pages inside, but what do I do? I start to darken them with ink.

12

As I write this, it's dusk already. Soon, about when I no longer see it, the words will begin to dissolve in it, the rising tide.

13

Imagine this: writing on a black page with white ink. And, just the shape of me, my shadow writing it.

14

My eyes hurt. Turn the page. I want to see what's written on the other side of light.

A Shadow on the House

where somebody died...
When you moved in, it was nothing
the neighbours would say; it was the shape,

precisely, left by their not-saying –
their not even saying a name,

that, and the fragments of hope
left behind, rainbow sticker askew
you started to unpeel from the window

then, no, that felt wrong. It was a darkening

you couldn't see, a mould stain on the soul
of bricks and mortar, where the shadow
soaked in. Fresh paint would not

conceal it; maybe a new love, new life, new
conception, if you had one, would. Or

give it houseroom; where else in the world
would have it? We are all strangers.
For now, it is more at home than you.

*

The stiller we stand
does that imprint our shadows deeper;

it's the settled sadness
that leaves traces, as much as the terrible act;

the ghost stories are wrong? Keep moving

and the negative imprinted
on the air, with each light-switch you click,

each way you turn,
is a flicker-book blur. You chasing you, you

then. As you were / as you are / as you were.

*

Or close your eyes; conceive of this: our shadows

are our guardians, tales of angels
as creatures of light
                              a deliberate diversion
so we look the other way.

It's not true that our shadows disappear
at night. They're released
                              like a breath. The whole
earth's shadow folds its wings around us,

all our weary fragments, debris of the day.

Crack and Warp

...as we all do, ageing.
　　Aching. Hand, eye, practised care
and chainsaw have carved us a companion
for the journey. Where
　　　　　I go, it says, you will go too.

*

Tree
　　cut to its essence, cross
between a barcode label and a ghost,

waits in the empty room
　　　　　　for time outside
to shift and lay a stripe of sun along it. Then

the air will fill with leaves, wind in them,
flicker-light, the shudder-by,
too quick to turn and see,
　　　　　　of birds.

*

Any day, in the crowd, in the queue,
it stands amongst us, alongside.
It could pass for a bare stump. No,

it is the kind of an angel
that's merely a thing when you look

but is human, more than, charged with presence
in the corner of your eye.

*

From the moment it came, the trunk shaved,
squared off roughly, bark and growth-wood stripped,
it has been leaving,

playing all parts in this parting scene:
the thin figure, receding, no one but its shadow
following; also the signpost at the wayside, and the tree

beneath which we might rest (although
it has no branches)
in the distant memory of shade.

*

As if a tree grew not
                leaves outwards but
unseen membranes of sensing
in to its own heart.
                As photosynthesis
drinks sunlight, so they reach for nourishment
from inward dark.

*

A totem pole
                of in-turned faces:
in each parallel slice, its whole
self coded, rings, knots, fractures, flaws.
Its privacy
                is not withholding
but a gift, a calm un-implicating grace
less like a body (though it holds the body's
every flinch and tremor)
                than a standing soul.

*

Slice by slice into but never through the heartwood,

        cut, till the trunk (it almost aches
to say this) is a spinal column... Year by year it dries
        and buckles into scoliosis (I know

whereof I speak) as if long wincing from a blow
        that may be older than this one life
set in early and became a habit of the bones.

*

It's a passage of wood that knows itself, you might say
        inwardly (each saw cut
a new surface, an inside outside and an outside in)

        the way no simply growing
thing does – in those fine seams, body-memories
        we can't decode but air can,

oxygen, moisture, patient scholars, reading at a depth
        by which the text itself is changed.

*

The fear, too, in these darkened corridors
of meeting the mind
                lost
among its echoes. Worked-out levels,
where a creak, a cough, a pick
                        dropped
could be right behind you, or years distant
like...
        you know, what's his name? His face
like yours. What was I about to say?

*

67

A verse form made from wood –
see the parallel lines, the artfully
shaved endings, the regular measure

disturbed, as it should be,
by the living breath. Cracks

open, midline, caesurae.
Cantilevered stresses in the grain
like night cramps. Hear all this,

in no time and without a single word.

*

Bare thing, stripped of its tropes,
its 'dancing in the wind'. Pure wood,
not word.
            And yet its stillness is
a dancing inwards. Lorca saw

the 80-year-old *bailaora* simply
stand –
            duende – and
the crowd struck dumb,
beyond breath, or applause.

('Crack and Warp', sculpture by David Nash)

If Today...

was the day, and this moment
    the moment before...
                    if the way
the new-washed sunlight
    zings back off the wall

with its flaky emulsion, its need
    for a lick and a promise
which it won't get now...
    if this was all
    the time there was...how suddenly

sun and someone's windscreen
    in Visitors Parking conspire
to mark that spot, just there
    with a brilliant
        blister of light,

and the shadow of that cable,
    unclipped, loops, with all
the necessary grace
    of a trapeze artiste's flight...
    if this was the wall

at the end of things, that scrape
    or patch of mould a hieroglyph,
calligraphy, a final statement, praise song for
    our work and care...
        what would I see

now, as clear as your face
    in my mind's eye
(as somebody's ring tone chirps and won't
    be answered)
        if this was the moment before?

Springtime in Pandemia

1 *Springwatch in Lockdown*

Birdsong in the human quiet. Streets
empty enough to walk through the middle of town
and step aside when one car comes in sight.

If Sunday, say, or New Year's Day is benchmark:
calm, then this is a minus reading.

Peacefulness below the level of comfort,
the dial on Danger... Now,
what would that be called?

*

As if in the pause of us, Spring is beginning.
As if it had been waiting
for us to be somewhere else...

Only, somewhere else, a place
called Elsewhere, has turned up to stay:

here, estranged, or us estranged in it.

And all of this is peaceful; anxious;
itchy on the surface of itself.

We long to scratch it. Are forbidden to.

*

A word from a single
cotyledon in the cracked path:

you had no idea, it says,
how fast everything could change.

You have no idea – just sit in there
and watch; I am the slightest

part of it – just how much more it could.

*

If I could match the deftness – the way
the play-chase-and-squabble of two adolescent rats

on the patio twines with their twitch-
perfect nose for a new chance, and the Spring-

loaded life force that catapults them off,
a slithering tight braid

of here-and-gone-ness, into cover,
their whisker-fine grip

on the balance of containment
and quest... well,

I would be a member of another species,
better suited maybe for the times we're in.

*

Nose to the grindstone
of a crisis – no,
to the plate glass window of it,

the thing, if single thing it is,
too close and wide to see –

only to see through, see
the way I see through glasses
with my face mask on – our breath

too hot, fogging the pane,
so we see little but the misting: our

own worry-sweat turning to chill
in every droplet. Finger-scribe
some big blunt letters in it; write

S P R I N G . Watch them pucker
and begin to weep. As if they cared.

2 *Pandemia*

It used to be a dream, the world
connected, commonwealth of breath,
        every border or wall,
however prickling with watchtowers and surveillance,

dissolved – all willed rifts, say,
between an island and its continent,
        made quaint
as the etiquette of an Archduke's hunting lodge.

Now, a knock on the door in the night:
the figure hooded by the streetlight,
        bone-face,
holding out that gift... What shall we say?

The state of All-Peoples: *Pandemia*.
One citizenry, with our different dialects
        of distance.
Could it have reached us any other way?

3 *The Straits*

Somewhere in the straits

between the names of pleasure beaches,
promenades avid with souvenir booths,

the cruise ships are stalled,

their engines idling, afterlives already
furnished with precise and petty luxuries,

the torment of all you ever asked for

served up to the (locked) door
of your cabin, echelon on echelon

of single windows. Look: the far

and tiny cities or, mostly, the sublime
no-comment of horizon. The unbroken sea.

while through the heating system's hum,

ducts, pipes, the million miles
of ageing arteries,

the speck of shadow spreads.

If we could see each other
we could count. The captain

on the tannoy is a thousand miles away.

4 *In the Light of the Times*

as when a low sun undercuts the cloud-mass,
startling the house fronts opposite too bright against
its slate-blue-grey, like stage-flats, operatic, slightly shuddering...

in the light that's no light we can see,

infra-red that conjures us as heat-ghosts,
the body's visible unconscious, our pulsing life-warmth
in the under-dark, leaving touch-tracks and smears as we fade....

in light that's more like darkness,

like the shrivelling cool gaze of x-rays
staring through the soft and moist, going straight
for the nub of us: tissues recomposing, growth, decay...

in the light of the facts

in which we ebb and eddy, nodes of data, a digital
balance unknown to ourselves... So we troop through the sidelines
of plague, old Totentanzers: look, my lords, the merry, dancing bones.

5 *This Quiet,*

a great stalled machine,
the one that we live beneath,
amongst the workings like mice in a mill...
          (Half true: we *are*

the workings: our desires,
consuming habits, blind eyes turned,
are what turns; the scrabblings and squeals
          between the floorboards

are our minds.) This quiet –
can we creep out now, or now? –
is disquiet: any moment, a jolt and a groan
        of jammed gears; the place

will shake, the mechanism
judder like a stopped heart shocked
awake. And that groan of newly tensioned metal,
        meshing round us,
                        sounds a lot like pain.

6 *Aside*

Even the crisis has an adolescence
when it thinks it can change the world,
when it's the only story. Then, like all of us,
the years of living with itself...

7 *The Morning After, Waking,*

from... What? The world was all there,
as is, but every distance between us was huge.
And yet we seemed to see things,
and each other, clearer than before:

how we would pass in the street,
each re-enacting the biblical 'pass by
on the other side'... but with a nod,
an un-committing smile, a curtsey in the dance,

here-I-am-there-are-you,
the radical equality, when each might
just be carrying (we always are)
our own, each other's, death

or sustenance; when the see-through
shelf-stacker in Tesco, only noticed before
as something in your momentary way,
or the driver easing down his lorry's tail-lift

with its slow leaky-lung wheeze,
might be a ministering sub-angel. (Not
one of the shining grand ones, true,
but what price anybody's grandeur now?)

The morning we'll wake, blinking,
wondering which was truer,
that dream, or the dream before,
called Normal – all we had believed

would be for ever. Superstitions. Waking,
maybe, in a clarity that takes our breath away
with choice. A moment on the threshold,
if we dare to see.

Descants on Dante

1 *The Lucifer Event*

The crash. The rupture. And the numbness after.
A shudder through time. The planet's history
is trauma: landmasses buckle, fracture and drift. Or

there's a stray jag of space-rock – a momentary
rip in the air, the earth itself a flinching
body. Long ash winter, and things freeze.

No fancy, then, to figure it as violation –
Lucifer's plunge, stabbed deep, like shrapnel
lodged close to the heart. The ocean

flash-boiling away. An unfathomable
void a whole hemisphere shrinks from. Then
the wounded magma gushes up to fill

the great unsaying: an island more fire than
rock at first, then steaming basalt. Mute
buttresses. Meanwhile a splinter-thin

wrongness, rusty skewer through the meat
of us, remains, an abscess, scar tissue
sealing it in like what a child might

still not find words for, groping through
a forty-year night. All you feel is a chill
from the chasm, like touching vertigo.

Don't look down. There is circle on circle
down there, souls' endless repetition
of themselves, worlds turning on a spindle

not of iron, not flame, but cold – a frozen
lake, a wind that locks the ice tears
to our eyes, words to our lips. Negation

itself, all hunger, and the null of gravity.
Almost absurd, the monstrous figure at the core
wedged upside down, now that we come to see.

2 *The Shores of Purgatory*

No word from the wind in the reed-beds, though it's all
voice, maybe all voices, in-folded/unfurled
like a bird flock. Murmuration. No wonder each soul

put ashore stands speechless. Where in the world
did the hymns they had been chanting to the bare horizon
go, lost in this white noise: surf-mist, wild-

fowl simmering into flight at their intrusion?
Distance... Who is saved enough for such
great openness? Their sentence: transportation.

Crimes? They'll spend the years unpicking which
of the wrongnesses was which, like oakum.
Old rope. If they've been a cargo, now each

is alone, with a horizon so wide and unbroken
you can see the earth's curve. Dry sand hisses
between marram. Slowly, creek-pools darken,

dreaming the sky back with the tide. A whisper-
thrill of a gust moves in among, becoming,
reed-wash. Was hope meant to look like this,

or to sound like the sweep of oystercatchers running
their touch down the edge of the wind, to test
its sharpness, while the sea is broken, undone,

done again? World without end. The taste
of salt on the soul's tongue. Sense by sense
they feel themselves dispersing, spreading, teased

apart in the simmer and surge, all difference
fading. No wonder that they have to turn away
to face the rock, raw magma-spill no plants

can root on, but familiar – it looks like pain –
and start to climb. The sea's huge gentle call
to ceaselessness came too soon. It won't come again.

3 *The Shadows of Paradise*

Beyond this point words shrivel, on the edge
of ignition. Still, they're all we have to go on
in this crescendo of light. But turn the page;

the marks show through: glyphs of unknowing,
read from the inside out. The inward twin
of speech is silence, light's is shadow; un-

things have their paradise. Somewhere between
the sixth and seventh heaven, it opens: you slip
through a crack, down, in, among the cogs that turn

the great device of light. How could God sleep
between creating days but in His darknesses?
You can have too much glory. Quiet as the lap

of waves on sand, here, angels of unspokenness,
of listening, like good parenting that knows
when to leave space, to say less

but reads the quietness eagerly as news,
mechanic angels, patient night-attendants,
ease the cogs and gears so that the epiphanies,

the great combustions, can whirl in the gravity dance
pouring their nuclear hearts out. Here, the peace
of being, its introspection, here, the Countenance

turned inwards, eyes closed, to feel the precise
touch of things – of skin, of moist soil, root-hairs,
fingertip to fingertip, of photosynthesis

like grace, God's subtlest metaphors,
the highest mathematics, the amoeba's
quivering one into two; touch that restores

the memory of ocean – one night in particular
so still the sea and sky seemed to exchange
reflections. Shoals of silences, the stars.

Thirteen Angels

What is the knocking?
What is the knocking at the door in the night?
Is it someone come to do us harm?

No, no, it is the three strange angels.
Admit them, admit them.

D.H. LAWRENCE,
'Look, We Have Come Through'

Of Breath

The angel of breath pays you a visit,
every other second. Don't look for it outside;
it has already entered you,

your pink and glistening cavities, though
the windpipe, through the branching bronchioles,
as they frill out and spread

then fold back into themselves,
the way the day-long haggling of a rookery
will settle in the high trees for the night.

The nearest you will come to wings,
it comes and goes between you and the air,
bringing back the good tidings

that a body waits for – oxygen
in the lingo of things, in other words,
in rough translation: life.

The angel visits; a voice can shudder awake,
step to the body's window-ledge
and, briefly, fly.

*

The Sublime

Come the day – the revolution or
the resurrection –
                          won't we all be changed?
As if the kettle's heart-glug after all its labour,
as if its final glottal click
was for this –

the release of an almost man-
sized twist of steam,
                          faint genie, djinn
kin to the dust-devils that practise all day
on the dance-floor of the desert...
This morning, a rare

beam through the kitchen window holds it
in its twenty seconds'
                          grand appearance
as in footlights, stepping through the curtain
of the night before

from the already half-forgotten play,
to glow;
              God's disposable angel
bodied just enough, in diffuse molecules,
to catch the light

then come apart in ordinary day –
no matter,
                it was charged with this:
to leave the air unbothered,
light unhindered.

Really, that was all it came to do.

*

A Glassy Thing,

an angel – quite see-through, exquisitely ground.
     Like a lens. What you see
is not it but through it, world refracted, clarified.
Follow it now
    down the street,
cut left behind the pound shop. Here it speaks
     in sprayed tags. Up the fire escape.
Here, on the long concrete landing. Here, gazing out
at the view. Roofs,
     roofs. Here, magnifying,
the small change of a life held up to catch
     the gift of light. Or it throws
us into long perspective, without warning;
we grow
    microscopic. Or
it climbs inside the mirror and looks back at you.
   Don't try to clutch it. It
might shatter, and the splinters of it cut you
     to the quick.

*

One Common Mistake

is to think that they are rare,
the angels. The maths of it beg (yes,
even logic can beg, faced with our cussedness)
     to disagree.
It's at the interfaces they appear –
between us, each and each other
and each and the tumult of things:
     the anthill's

towering, tart-smelling intellect,
the inaudible growl of the grass
as it gets its claws into everything, the virus
                              singing its oh-
so-catchy one song in our blood,
and bins, and half-bricks, every surface
that could catch a glint of the light, or vivid
                              darkness – don't
start counting. Even God
doesn't have time for that, although
the angels of the shifting in-between-ness,
                              each glistening
connective thread, each wink
of serendipity – the weave of it and not
the rattling bits of our separate selves –
                              might be all that He sees.

*

An Angel is a Kind of Music

not that of the spheres but of the here and now,
their frictions,
                              as small boats hauled up the slipway,
on the sea wall, in a rising wind,

convene a gamelan from their slack rigging – how
the same wind's brush
                              across an uncapped drain
calls up the first deep-in-the-ribcage quivering

before the huff of panpipes, as if blown cloud
came freighted not
                              with the onset of rain
but memory of mountains. Let them in,

these passing angels, and they'll crowd
the hallway;
                    you may never sleep again.
The least creak on the stairs, and they'll sing.

*

The Angel of Flow

spreads the tips of her/his being up, out, as wide
as the valley, its filaments into the clefts,

the rattling gullies or into the acid memories
of peat. A day of rain, the muscle flexes;

glossy, feathering out, you hear it start to tremble,
then to beat.
                    And: the angel of flow

condenses, smoothing wings back slick
against a sinuating body, frilled for fine tuning,

to camber, as he or as she, round the slaloms
of force, silver-plated with scales and concentration.

Now, like a plucked string of light. Now, plunged deep
into herself; and now, quivering upstream

against gravity. Should you catch her by accident,
throw her back. You might as well go fishing for a river.

A minute or two of gasping, struggling, feebler,
and she's merely fish.

*

The Angel of the Inconsistency

of things
           can be relied on,
in his way. Don't trust me, he says
and you'd better believe him

even though
           or is that because
he's a self-contradiction. Just like you,
he says, and he tips you that slippery

half-smile
           you catch sometimes
on your own reflection – never full-face
in the mirror. Just as you're turning away.

*

I Am Here to Begin,

said this one, on the deconstruction.
He didn't look like a builder. Nor an academic. Hold on,

I said, I think you've got the wrong address.
He shook as weighty and awfully balanced a head

as a lighthouse's glittering lens-array
afloat on silence, on its bath of mercury –

I'll give him credit for the hesitation.
No, no, not the house... He looked me up and down

to the blood, to the bone,
                and I knew.

*

Of Emptiness

The angel of emptiness – yes,

consider s/he too might be an angel
though s/he feels like just the opposite;

she might be here to upturn your idea of an angel –

also exerts power on time and space.
Not by charging them with meaning. Just the opposite.

This too is an awesome thing,

for time to be all one same un-advancing tick,
for any step in space to be towards horizons

you can't ever reach or look beyond.

The angel of dark matter:
the untallied burden of the universe,

that which disables all our snug equations,

matter not behaving as it should. I'd say
the empty angel sits at God's right hand,

in almost all the universe, except there is

no right, or left, or handedness, there is no place,
unless it's everywhere, where she sits.

*

The Angel of the Slight

and Almost – of the least rank, below
the Dominions, the Powers, the Thrones:

the Nuances, the angels of fine tuning,
of each, any, moment in its balancing

along the Bridge of One Hair; one petal,
oyster-pink, tipped from the climbing rose

to fall, under mere weight of sunlight; the melt
of one snowflake that begins the avalanche –

the most quietly militant of angels, in their minute
near-imperceptible rebuttal of the brag and bray

of big simplicity, its marching orders. Angel of the caught
breath, of the comma or the careful line break or

small word, barely bearing a meaning, that marks,
that makes, a change in the momentum of the world.

*

Who'd Have Thought

the debris of those unregarded lives,
the words choked in their throats,
their fluent silences bricked in by noise,

could constitute an angel?
But look at the stress lines spreading
through the concrete at your feet,

cracks feathering, flexing, dust-flakes
crumbling, as it rises; the crackling
sound as it fills out its wings.

The first downbeat is clumsy;
it gathers its mass, bundled armfuls of flight,
and flings it. The horizons shudder

like the tacky backdrop we half knew
they were. It clears its throat
like white noise, like a waterfall, like wind.

*

A Latter-Day Angel

To know that one is late
in the day, to feel it slipping away

with the sun, after its brilliant inquisitions
into the matter of things

like next door's ash tree at my window,
with its fresh leaves and its twig-tips withering

with Dieback, read out like a barcode label
on my bedroom wall through the crack in the blinds;

to see the world turned, and time with it,
in God's hand, but nothing passing –

this is just the shape of Always,
globe-like – and you on it, there in this age,

in the shape of your ageing, turned in a gaze
that sees from every angle, with a glint

on it, here and there, and shadows...
To know this, to know it whole,

might have to be postponed until a later
angel comes. Till then, one has to wait.

*

The Thirteenth Angel

                not so much the uninvited
     at the christening as the one
there are no words for in the language.

                Not even a space in the air.
     Say my name, says the nothing
but day upon day rushes in; the lack seems

                to be filled. And yet.
     Try to speak, you taste it, the shock
of animal intimations, something rotting

                in the roadside thicket, bad
     news, the stink that has a sweetness
on its breath; feel the weight of humidity, here

                inside you, like a raincloud
     on the x-ray, on the conscience,
in the small hours, in the margins of the soul.

                In fifty years, too late
     for you, this will all seem so clear;
the thirteenth angel will have written the page

                on which you're a name
     or less, a hyperlink that clicks
into the mist. Today, though, it's here, its silence

        like a gift for something raw,
    pink, crying, oh, unreasonably
into being. And the thirteenth angel is the world itself.

Silence Like Rain

Silence, like rain, falling
on the Quaker meeting, on the congregation
of rooks at the edge of the wood, on the *sangha*
where a young monk enters late, at the back, folds his saffron robe in place
a little too carefully, then even he forgets himself

in silence, like rain falling, spreading
West, like evening, over fens dark with the bad
dreams of prehistory, rain spreading out in fans, flared wings
of rufflement across grey sea like the grey of the sky with wind visible;
silence falling on deep forest,

pine and spruce accepting it
like their own in-breath, silence as particular
in detail and uncountable as the pine needles; falling evenhandedly
on drought and rising flood, tapping windows as we tap-tap the barometer,
the long-range forecast, nagging questions;

silence falling on the just and unjust,
like a blessing on parched fields, like a thrill
of recognition, an astonishment of welcome raising
petrichor, the savour of new-wetted earth; elsewhere, equally, a weight
of loneliness, shouldered daily; a family curse

falling into a pale child's locked room,
the name of the lock, Our Little Secret; storm drains
overflowing, a choked gush roiling up; rain on a crowded market,
in a drench at the first gunshot, just before the screaming; silence drowned
by an absence of sound so loud with power

and prohibition that we're dumbed;
sometimes we have to cry out for true silence again;
a steady downpour darkening the pavement, muddying the sky;

falling at last after centuries of more and more elaborate rain-dances,
all found wanting, falling as a gift;

silence disguised as music,
not the notes, the five, six strands of voices buttressed
one against each other in the high vault Thomas Tallis built
but the echoing space between them, vast enough that clouds form
in the rafters, fine rain falling, silence falling

through the shredding veils of sound; rain
so clear and minute, if you could live up close enough
to see, it's almost nothing, and never the same drops falling
yet a whole world reflected in each, so many that what can our minds
say but 'the same'; silence like rain

dissolving riverbanks, distinctions
between what is sound and what its opposite;
that can crispen our hearing to a shock of definition and
can loosen us, to nothing but itself; a silence that's a speaking
that is its own listening,

that gradually confides: this is nothing
to do with the absence of sound; a silence that dispenses
with itself, that shucks off 'silence' like its dry husk, the word
and the thought of it; that makes us a place in the world; silence fed
like rainfall from a cycle too vast

and slow to see except in glimpses,
say, the cloud-piles building on the sea horizon,
heavy with the future, weather, coming. Silence
that is our whole habitation, here-ness, how this water-planet
thinks and breathes and speaks.